BLAST OFF!

A SPACE COUNTING BOOK

by Norma Cole   illustrated by Marshall Peck III

ini Charlesbridge

For Andrew, who asked questions — NC

For Franquin and Hergé — MHP III

Published by Charlesbridge
85 Main Street, Watertown, MA 02472 • (617) 926-0329
www.charlesbridge.com

Library of Congress Cataloging-in-Publication Data
Cole, Norma
    Blast-off!: a space counting book / by Norma Cole; illustrated by
Marshall Peck III.
        p.   cm.
    ISBN-13: 978-0-88106-499-5 (reinforced for library use)
    ISBN-10: 0-88106-499-8 (reinforced for library use)
    ISBN-13: 978-0-88106-498-8 (softcover)
    ISBN-10: 0-88106-498-X (softcover)
    1. Counting—Juvenile literature. 2. Astronomy—Juvenile literature.
[1. Counting. 2. Outer space. 3. Solar system.] I. Peck, Marshall H., ill.
II. Title.
QA113.C64   1993
513.2'11—dc20
[E]   93-28794
                                                                  CIP
                                                                   AC

Printed in Korea
(hc)   10 9 8 7 6 5 4 3 2
(sc)   10 9 8 7 6

Zero

Would you like to be a space traveler?
Let's go!

For years, people have been trying to understand what they see up in the sky, in that vast area that we call space. In the night sky, we can see the distant stars and planets, but wouldn't it be great to go up there? Imagine being an astronaut!

1 One

In the 1960's, the first astronauts had to wear space suits and shoes with magnets to hold them down. Space suits were made of fifteen layers of material to keep the correct pressure inside. All those layers and heavy shoes made it hard to move. Imagine wearing ten-pound shoes, fifteen shirts, and fifteen pairs of pants at the same time!

Two

Buckle your astronaut shoe.

Now, we control the pressure inside a spaceship so that astronauts can wear regular clothes. They wear space suits only when they leave the ship to walk in space. Astronauts are weightless in space because there is so much less gravity than there is on Earth. They must learn how to walk and float around, and they have to tie themselves down when they go to bed!

Spaceships carry a supply of air for the astronauts to breathe because there is no air in space. You cannot see, smell, or taste air, but it has pressure and weight. Inside a spaceship the air is kept at about 15 pounds of pressure because that is what people need to breathe comfortably.

Four

Close the spaceship door.

Since the air pressure inside a spaceship is so high and the pressure outside is almost zero, the doors have to be built very carefully. To leave a spaceship, astronauts have to go through an area between two doors called an air lock. If there were no air lock, the moment somebody opened the door, all the air would be sucked out of the ship.

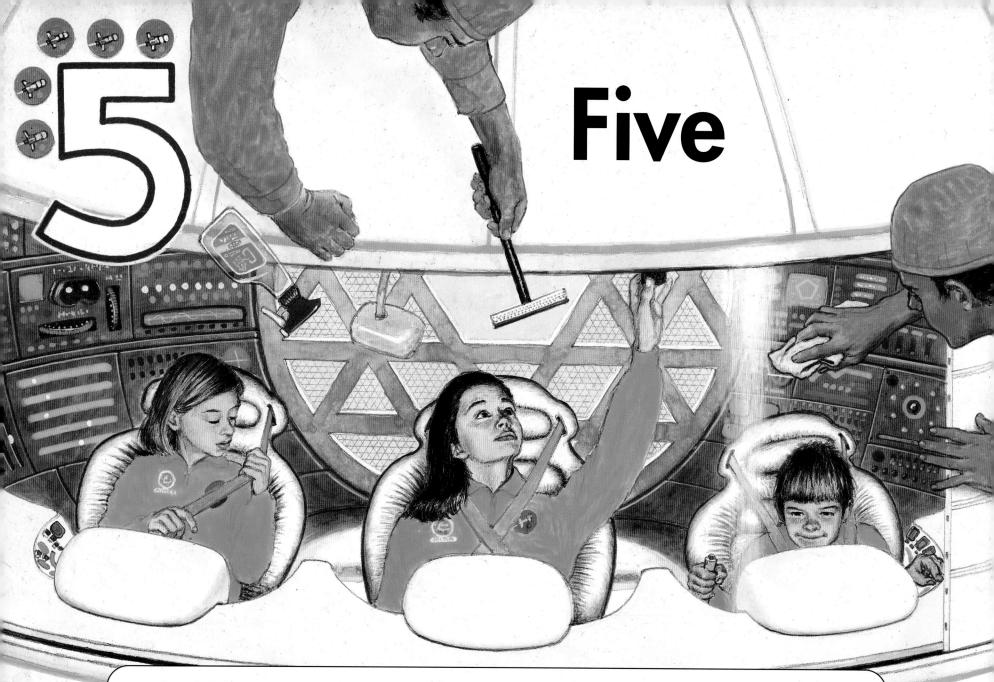

The tools we normally use to find our way around on Earth do not work in space. A compass, for example, only works in Earth's magnetic field. Also, there are no signs or landmarks in space to steer by.

Six

Use the guiding stick.

6

Astronauts can use the Sun, the planets, and groups of stars called constellations to find their way around in space. The star closest to us, Alpha Centauri, is 4.3 light years away. A light year is the distance light travels in a year or 5,878,000,000,000 (5 trillion, 878 billion) miles.

7 Seven

We launch spaceships into space with rockets. Rockets are really just large tubes filled with explosives. When a rocket is started up, it makes explosions beneath it. These explosions push the rocket up into space. Once in space, rocket blasts are used only for changing direction.

Eight

Set the flight path straight.

8

The Moon is the closest object to Earth. The Moon moves in a circular orbit, or path, around the Earth at 2,000 miles per hour! To land on the Moon, the astronauts must head for the place where the Moon will be in several days.

9
Nine

Look how high astronauts can jump on the Moon! That is because the Moon's gravity is so weak. If you weighed 85 pounds on Earth, you would only weigh 14 pounds on the Moon. So far, people have traveled only as far as the Moon. We have sent out remote-control cameras to take pictures so that we can see what a trip into space would be like.

Ten *Blast off!*

No one has yet been to a planet other than Earth. A planet is something that circles or orbits a sun. There are nine planets in our solar system. Each one can have more than one moon. Sometimes it is possible to see planets at night. They look like stars except they do not twinkle.

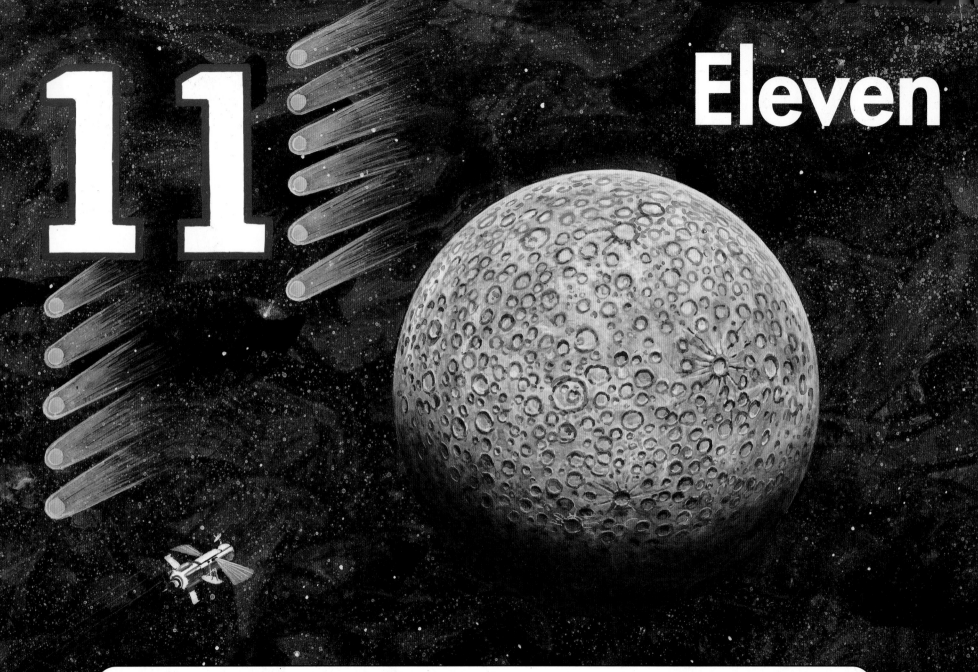

11

Eleven

If we went into space, we might swing by Mercury, the closest planet to the sun. It makes one complete orbit around the sun in only 88 days. The time it takes a planet to orbit the sun is what we call a year. The surface of Mercury is rocky and has lots of giant holes called craters. Mercury was named for the fast-moving messenger in Roman mythology.

Twelve

12

See the planets
for ourselves!

Venus is a very hot planet. It is covered by clouds of carbon dioxide, the gas we breathe out. This gas acts like a blanket and keeps heat beneath it. On the surface of Venus it is hot enough to melt metal!

Earth is the third planet from the Sun. It is where we live. Two thirds of Earth's surface is covered with water. That is why it looks blue. Hundreds of years ago, people used to think that the Moon, the Sun, the planets, and all the stars revolved around Earth. Now we know that the planets in our solar system revolve around the Sun.

Fourteen

What a beautiful scene!

Have you ever seen shooting stars? They are actually chunks of rock called meteors that are burning up as they approach Earth. When you see something that looks like a slow-moving star, it is probably a satellite that scientists have sent up to orbit Earth. Once every 76 years, you might see Halley's comet. A comet is made of gas and ice. It has a bright, fuzzy head and a tail.

15

Mars is called the red planet because it is covered with red sand. The sand is red because it is full of rusty iron. Two oddly shaped moons circle this planet. Mars has many long channels that people once thought were canals filled with water. We now know that the only water on Mars is frozen on its north and south poles.

Sixteen

16

Fly around and in between.

Jupiter is the largest planet in the solar system. It has more than 16 moons! Jupiter is so large that more than 1,000 Earths could fit inside it. Most of Jupiter is gas. Scientists think that the solid core of Jupiter is made of coal. It is possible that the core of Jupiter is a giant diamond!

17 Seventeen

Saturn is the second largest planet in the solar system but it weighs very little. Saturn would float in water if you could find an ocean it would fit in. Saturn's rings are made up of ice and dust. The ice and dust form lumps that can be as small as a grain of sand or as large as a truck.

Eighteen

Find things we've never seen!

18

Uranus is a strange planet. It has rings like Saturn's but not as large. Uranus is turned on its side so that each pole of the planet faces the sun and is light for half of the year while the other pole is dark.

19

Nineteen

Neptune is a very cold planet. Of its several moons, Triton is the largest. Triton has volcanoes that spit ice instead of fire. One moon, Nereid, orbits counter-clockwise, which is backwards for a moon.

Twenty

This is as far as we want to be.

20

Pluto is the last planet in our solar system. It is so far away from the sun that one year on Pluto is 248 years long on Earth. Pluto's orbit is strange, too. Sometimes it is the farthest planet from the sun, and sometimes it is not!

10 Ten

20 Twenty

30 Thirty

40 Forty

50 Fifty

60 Sixty

70 Seventy

80 Eighty

90 Ninety

100 One Hundred

How many stars can you see?

A star is made of giant clouds of hydrogen gas. Gravity pulls the gas into a ball and then starts shrinking it. As the ball gets smaller, it heats up inside and gets brighter. Eventually the heat pushes out enough to stop the ball from getting smaller, and the ball becomes a star. Our Sun is a star. It looks big because it is much closer than the other stars.

1,000   one thousand

10,000   ten thousand

100,000   one hundred thousand

1,000,000   one million

1,000,000,000   one billion

1,000,000,000,000   one trillion

There are so many stars!

The light given off by stars takes years to reach Earth, so when we see a star in the sky, we are actually seeing how it looked many years ago. Gravity tends to hold millions of stars together in groups called galaxies. Our galaxy forms a spiral shape called the Milky Way.

Are you ready to go back to Earth?

Begin the countdown!

The length of a day is different on each planet. One day and night on Earth is 24 hours because that is how long it takes our planet to turn, or rotate on its axis, one time. Each planet turns around at a different speed, so its day is a different length.

10 Ten

Nine 9

Check the clock for time.

Perhaps, in the future, when people live on other planets, we will need to invent a special, new word for a day on Earth, and other new words for a day on Mars, a day on Venus, and so on. To help us talk about space, we have already invented some new words such as light year, space shuttle, escape velocity, and spaceport.

8 Eight

Seven 7

Some people call space *heaven*.

In ancient times, people thought that there was a dome over the Earth like a bowl turned up-side-down over a dish. Now we know that space is much bigger than that. No one knows just how big it is. The word for limitless time and space is infinity.

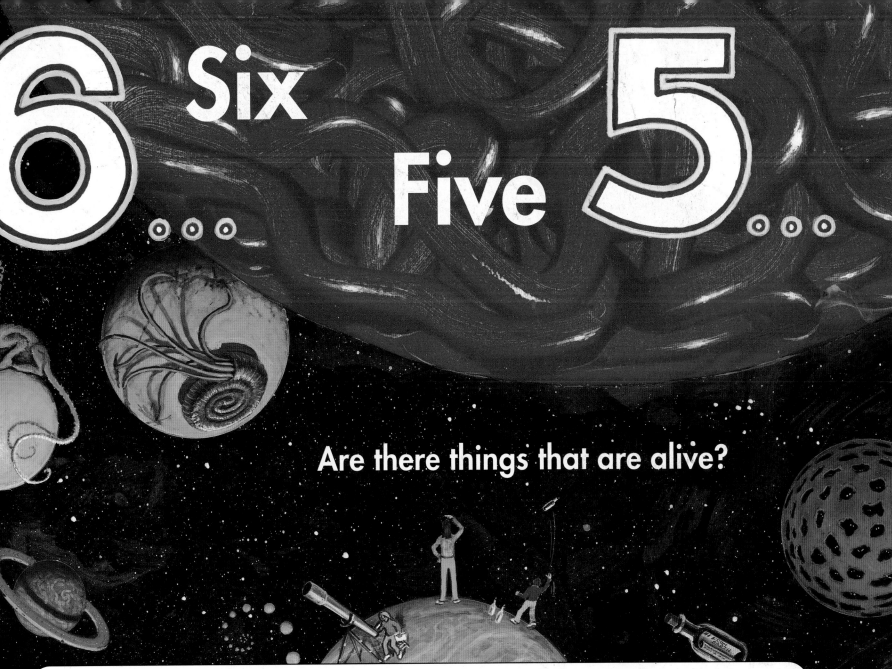

6 Six Five 5

Are there things that are alive?

As far as we know, the only living creatures are on Earth. We have sent messages into space to see if any life forms might respond. Our message has a picture of what humans look like, and a record saying, "Hello" in many languages. Right now, scientists are trying to communicate using radio wave messages. What do you think an ET (extraterrestrial) would look like?

4... Four Three 3...

This is the life for me!

Astronauts not only have to run the spaceship, but they also have to do many other tasks. They have to do experiments, clean the ship (not easy without gravity), eat, sleep, exercise, and talk with people on Earth. Life in space is an exciting challenge!

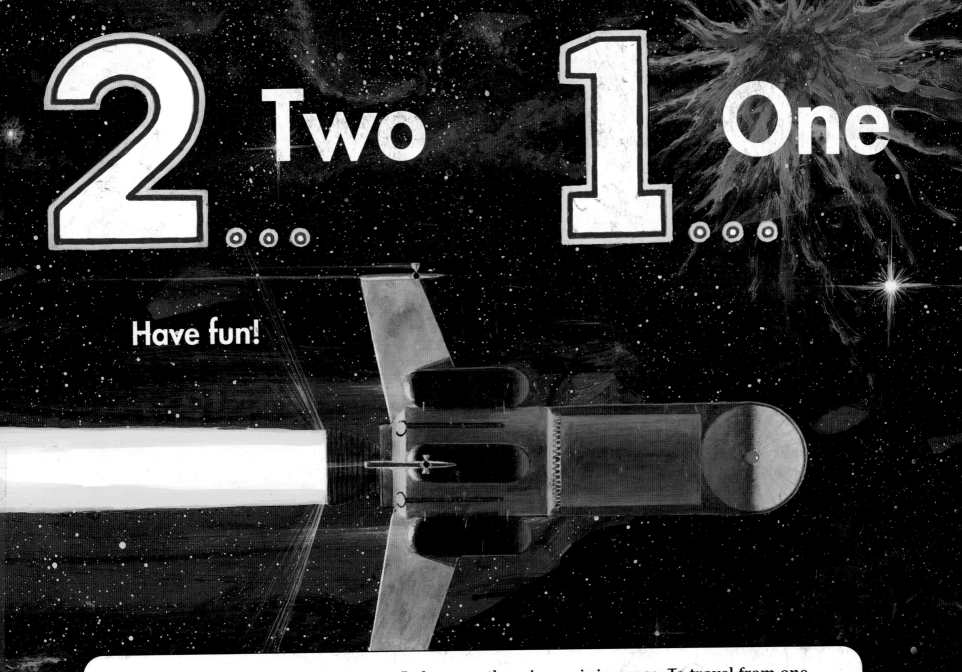

2... Two

Have fun!

1... One

A spaceship does not need wings to fly because there is no air in space. To travel from one place to another, the astronauts merely turn the rocket engines on and coast to where they want to go. To stop, they put the engines in reverse.

O Zero

Maybe <u>you</u> can be a space hero!

There is so much about space that we still do not know. Just like the explorers on Earth long ago, space explorers may discover new and exciting places. Would you like to be a space explorer?